WHE
THERE
WAS
LIGHT

ALSO BY CARLIE HOFFMAN

This Alaska

WHEN THERE WAS LIGHT

POEMS

CARLIE HOFFMAN

FOUR WAY BOOKS

TRIBECA

Library of Congress Cataloging-in-Publication Data
Names: Hoffman, Carlie, author.
Title: When there was light / Carlie Hoffman.
Description: New York : Four Way Books, [2023] | Summary: "Carlie Hoffman -
    When There Was Light"-- Provided by publisher.
Identifiers: LCCN 2022033090 (print) | LCCN 2022033091 (ebook) | ISBN
    9781954245426 (paperback) | ISBN 9781954245433 (epub)
Subjects: LCGFT: Poetry.
Classification: LCC PS3608.O47753 W48 2023 (print) | LCC PS3608.O47753
    (ebook) | DDC 811/.6--dc23/eng/20220721
LC record available at https://lccn.loc.gov/2022033090
LC ebook record available at https://lccn.loc.gov/2022033091

This book is manufactured in the United States of America and printed on acid-free paper.

Four Way Books is a not-for-profit literary press. We are grateful for the assistance
we receive from individual donors, public arts agencies, and private foundations
including the NEA, NEA Cares, Literary Arts Emergency Fund, and the
New York State Council on the Arts, a state agency.

We are a proud member of the Community of Literary Magazines and Presses.

CONTENTS

I

II

III

IV

THE FUTURE HAS AN ANCIENT HEART.
—CARLO LEVI

Poem Ending in the Light

When I was suffering, I left Manhattan. *It's not good*
        for me here I wrote over and over on yellow Post-its.

There was a park I walked toward in the evenings, cautious
        to not cross through it to where you lived. I lived

with a painter who was obsessed with Atlantic City
        and the color blue, who was in love

with a married man from Virginia. We spent the summer
        broken-hearted among the green tomatoes.

a selfish girl a selfish girl a selfish girl
        I wrote, thinking of home, my mother at the window

with her life gone cold. The night I left I watched the bull
        speared above Earth, whole as grief, like a moon.

And like the moon I was drawing myself inside
        an unconditional orb of light.

Walking Without You in Riverside Park

Just beyond the chain-link
fence, the sycamores twist—
first away, then toward each other,
in a jagged row like a bloodline,

like a kind of love,
and can you blame
yourself for having loved
in that selfish, begging way

of the young?
It's important to walk like this:
through the places where the vanished
people of our lives

have walked, until it's time
to eat again, until all
that's left
to pick at

is fish skin
in the corner of a
dimly lit bar
till the candles cease.

Listening to Schumann's *Träumerei*

The last time I wake in the foreclosed house
a deer arrives faithfully in the yard.

Why is it all connected this way, suddenly
remembering your mustard coat

running through the park, a sun I followed.
I am sick and constantly in awe

of how easily the day spoils.
I am sick

and pull my hand through your hair
wishing to be out of my head.

Is childhood worth
remembering, I ask.

You are the deer
I know, punishing to touch.

Late Show

Summer where the sun steams
my mother's cotton dress
as she sits in lemongrass
sucking ice cubes and sweating
behind the house where mosquitoes
raid her skin. *You have sweet blood,*

my mother's mother says
pinning bed sheets to the brittle
clothesline, which startles
the bird-flecked trees
because she is more obsidian.

Your mother is a person you try
jumping in the same way you would
a glassy stream,
only to find it frozen. All summer

humid air thick as syrup,
the house empty, wooden clips
cradling the pillowcases. The past
a steamed-over kettle, you will spend
your life going back.

A Blessing

It seems to me a blessing now that my sister
came first, raging and reigning like a human
through the house, while our younger brother
and I crammed our bodies underneath the round
dining table, field mice entering a tulip's ear.
Her hair was thicker, darker, and her eyes
a hazy green, which made ours more brown,
more the same, soldiered, laughing in the front yard
while we watched our father chuck her boom box
out the bedroom window, laughing uncontrollably
as it bruised the driveway like a child's cheek
slapped in the middle of a freezing afternoon.
It was funny because we believed in the transaction
of retaliation—her broken music a reimbursement
for her control over the bedroom door (opened
or closed), for spitting in our faces.
It was a blessing she was the first girl, our father
holding her jaundiced, firstborn body toward
the ribbon of sunlight from the hospital's window
the first week of her life. This saved her, you know,
so when my brother and I chose to follow our mother
away from the burning field, she was bound to it.

A Decade After Looking
at My Father's Photo Album of Walter Reed
National Military Medical Center

My mother shuts the front door of the house

she doesn't own

and nods to the grass for the last time,

the radishes an oily flame she puts

on her lipstick in the dark.

My father, alone, drives through

the fresh wind

mumbling the *Ana beKo'ach*. He is religious now. His sister

went blind young.

His voice is the stray dog barking

at the snow, believing the little strawberries grow wilder

against a field.

I point to Russia on the map. I point to

Poland and Germany. It was

another time. My people

another time. The synagogues burn decades

of new snow. Then

America. My father in the picture. His olive

army hat. The photo album glowing

like a severed shoulder of a man.

This verging snow

it buries my mother and me. She shuts the front door.

Summer Brings No Cash I Quit

The suburban town off the highway I quit

the house ragging into oblivion the hostess stand I quit

I drop off menus one last time am a handful

of quits in the park I read the newspapers all about cold I quit cold I,

a consequence I run out of. I run out of clean underwear

clean hair rain comes I slam the door turn back. I quit

Shabbos quit Evelyn cutting

pictures wedding gown purple flower butchered

magazines pouring out: walls drawers laundry boiled potatoes
                                        chicken broth

I quit the bride—mouthed communal prayer

my beheaded tongue Hebrew tongue Russian tongue

I comprehend nothing know

nothing summer fevers the trees

the anxious fish no God is coming to quit.

While Waitressing at the Kosher Restaurant a Man Calls Me a Whore and a Woman Rushes Behind Me into the Kitchen to Hand Me Her Baby

Every season is good for killing girls,
        the seaweed-black night foaming

with stars—
        a plaque of women's names.

Before Mary's a whore,
        a baby is placed in the frozen bird

of her lap, the dignity in being.
        Every place that hurts you

is the season where the sun bursts
        like salmon on fire. Think

of Eve shivering naked beneath the alder
        watching God get angry—

is it anger or is it grief—all of us doing
        what we've been trained to do.

The Women Gather at Biala River at Night

Light sheds its skin in the poplars,
        Earth's soldiers wielding the dark, bats emerging

like machinery along the branches, a trick of the eyes,
        and still the river is a cantor, singing.

Once, in a holy city, all around me the women wept,
        craning their perfumed necks,

hooked fisheyes swelling in birdless light.
        Once, blood glimmered on the rocks here

in meager testimony. Not here, but inside here,
        within the cities within a story, soft framework

where loneliness flowers. Here, I go to the women, take
        forgiveness from their hands, drill

the bullet-sized hole in my head to receive
        the light in its endless repetition.

Once, light brushed the hair of my dead aunts as they bent
        to kiss their siddurs on the other side of the drought.

How their bodies grew wet as eels gathering
        underneath a sentence, mouthing gibberish,

an engine refusing to shut off, and inside,

what God will do when I die.

Yahrzeit in December

She is paranoid like my mother and me
when she answers my call
and responds *What do you really*
want, in tiny bursts in-between
pauses, and I could stand
relieved all afternoon in Brooklyn
in front of the butcher shop
tracing back the gene
of neuroticism that gorges
on a mind, and for the first time I love
how a blizzard comes down
in fractions, am completely
sure that December is the month
of remembering the dead

because today is the anniversary
of her brother's heart
eaten by the snow, which I don't speak of
because I can only say I am
her brother's granddaughter
and though we have never met
I need to know about the ship
that carried my bone math—the hind legs
of a lamb swaying in the butcher's
window that reflects my face
countering my face.

Calling Payne Whitney Psychiatric Clinic

February, worst month, blooms a flu beneath
your skull. You lie still on the mattress
and count your breath. Rain. Your body a wound

stuffed with sound. The person you love
has left: what you know of their voice:
a shock collar. As a child, zipped in a bright

yellow coat like a jessamine,
for stretches of winter, you lay still like this
on a bench at recess, the airwaves swelling

in your lungs, terrified
to be approached by the other children,
a rubber ball, or rope, ashamed you couldn't rise

until the whistle. You hear
the rain, bare, an abbreviation,
each drop on the roof like a tooth

capped with blood. On the line a voice
is a yellow field, even when
all February hours are taken, you believe

it is a field of raincoats
for no other reason
but your life.

Almost the Last of It

I've lost you again. The flag
went limp in the yard, last night's wind
a mad lover in the dark, then
gone, like wind. Then back,

in my old life, I'm standing
in your room
an invisible question rising in the throat.

I have a window with trees I can talk to
when I am sad. A good,

grief-woven language. Pink hibiscus
tonguing the side of the house.

End of February at the Market,
After a Panic Attack

All year the pigs hang by their ankles
        among the newspapers and plastic-wrapped

flowers, the days paused inside the curve
        of hairless ears, curled toes like nerve endings.

I promised I would walk to the park and stay
        until I was calm, but the wind stinks with an offering

from the ginkgoes. Yesterday, I watched a woman
        possessed by grief at the museum, her hand

floating toward a Van Gogh until security
        snapped her out of it, the crowd a purified gasp.

She didn't jerk her head in horror, just straightened
        her shawl, mumbling, *Oh*.

At the meat counter, the pig's eye is an integer for a stadium-lit
        field:
        stars like spiders stabbed above the track,

teenagers drunk and throwing glass, the metallic bark
        of them fucking beneath the bleachers.

How can I live on love alone?
        Spring is close, but how can I sleep

knowing they're out there

    awake all night, mouths wide open.

Give the Lake a Moment
to Speak About the Horses

I have a heart. It is full
    of horses. My mother's

heart, the horses.
    In the lake's center,

rain breathes down.
    Someone lies bedridden.

Someone's brother
    goes estranged. For years,

hooves steep in mud,
    a mare's bent knee.

Closure is the rain
    dripping over blood-lined leaves

above our dream lake. No,
    the water was never blue.

No, don't catch
    this heart. Sadness, too,

it carries. Which horse

      do you carry?

That's what you need to know.

Beyond Harm

I'm thinking incessantly
of the story my mother
repeated about
her twenties, how she
watched, silent
as a monk, as her father,
a good man in his bone
collar, became
a new font in the earth,
the farm which was
her inheritance
hacked like an apple
against his will.
All the living
men in my family
become thieves.
Don't be sad yet.
She will take
them to court and marry
my father, win
back the money.
Years later, he gambles
all her savings
away, the house
forecloses. My mother
leans against the cracked
screened door in navy

sweatpants beneath a pale
blade of light,
wondering how
old she's become.

On a Prewar Piano

From the future, I watch the lights
flickering in the windows of a boat.
Shivering in the icy weather of
another planet's sea, I wait silently
for its docking. Soon, people
with my bone structure step over
the threshold where I can see
their glowing ankles and briefcases
filled with news of the world.
The world has so many rooms it's
impossible to pinpoint where mine begins.
During the war, my grandfather
emerges from a ship and traces
his new alphabet across the dirt.
The ship's hull balloons
into an elephant-rubbed sky.
Soon the sky fills with people.
My grandfather turns the dial
of his American radio
to the prayer of a wordless song.

Grandfather Reading Celan in Middletown, NY

We walk the little Grove
Street Park that bleeds into North
Street, dirt clouding the cemented path,
a few blood-flushed leaves, relief, then snow.
Lord of this hour was a wintercreature. Each ghost
unspools from the cuticle between branches
as spiders down each web's spine. His brother's
ghost hovers by the stream with all the cousins
apologizing for never speaking plainly to each other:
fear of locked-in syndrome, palpitating hearts,
black milk in the blood, shame. Nobody wants a ghost,
but now the image of his brother
hanging from a rope in the rafters
is a prophecy in repose, and as he reads the translation
his *torn-awake vein knots itself,* the incredulous tongue
measures each split end. I want to meet
my grandfather at the beginning,
before the mothers in the market worry a finger across the stamp
on a milk jug, triple-checking the date. How untrustworthy
the mind, its longing of what it knows. How miserable
to relinquish our innermost parts
in service of the mind. I go astray in everything
but now I am rushing behind his grey coat
in the grizzled afternoon, eavesdropping. Something carved,
without extension, *my climbing mouth biting in.*

After the Farm was Sold to FedEx

My grandfather is still alive
and living upstate, smoking
on the porch with one leg up.
He's watching a cloud of boys
toss a baseball back and forth
with such grace and economy,
sneakers kicking dust
into apricot mouths,
sweating backs colorful and clawed.
He is watching them move
toward their most
primitive selves: flaming horses
in the old barbed-wire farm.
So much of what's been lost belongs
to the ground—
newspaper headlines, the family
name—all drunk
and dreamed away. Soon,
every voice around
wills the present tense.
Like their country's flag,
all the mothers wave dish towels
out the kitchen windows
for their sons to come inside
and wash their hands.
Wait, he says, and the wind
catches. The boys drop their mitts
offhandedly on the grass.

Ocean Liner to the United States, 1935

I.

Edelweiss petals ripped from their earthly stem,
how the night severs you

from your neighbors, all the look-alikes
jamming wooden trunks

crammed with bread and underwear
into the shining corners of temporary rooms.

It will rain soon, stinging rains anesthetizing
the sea's deep centuries, water overflowing,

elephant pools, like the Neisse pouring into
the Baltic. Air touches each sleeper

with woolly-leafed fingers as they dream
of the soft hurricanes of running feet.

II.

Nothing good comes from people,
            your sister says, her rope-thin
body swaying in the hyacinth dark.

Thousands of bodies West, you hear
            singing, imagine a creature
who is missing a human tongue

27

dancing indefinitely alone. In America
          someone asks a question about
hearing voices without mouths,

like a rootless tree
          floating above a stream.
Over and over

your sister braids the exhausted
          strands of her hair,
mumbling the hours.

III.

Within the laws of merging and parting
          a girl my grandfather loves is losing

his name, his face blurred
          by the freezing winds.

In the midst of war, before
          battle cry & gunpowder & *feindliche Truppen* &

enemy position & ambush & body count,
          before the blood we drink

from the river, there are the laws
          of merging and parting, the law

in which, because he is Jewish,
          the girl my grandfather loves, pretty,

shiny as a missile in her uniform

       on the way to school, plucking

orange blossoms, remains *eine Mädchen*

       while he becomes the wind.

IV.

Mother imagines birds in her sleep:
white stork, heron, their migration patterns
weaving throughout her temporal lobes, enduring
wings pumping steadily against cold air
as though pushing northern temperatures
toward the back of a giant closet at their will.

*

(During an earthquake in a new century
sixteen snowy egrets are hurled
from a split tree like baseballs
and live.)

*

Simple to make a metaphor
out of birds. Wrong metaphor.
We knock on the closet door
and the door opens to a century
of sky and centuries of centuries
of sky. Which is to say to nothing
and no one.

Like Television

The West would teach me to wake
in the clouded dawn and open

a giant freezer to chop meat
for the barn dogs, mottled geese

going berserk in the yard, my
little sister snoring ferociously

in the amethyst hour.
My adolescence—

ruled by sound and walls
full of horse hair. There I am:

raking mulch in a drizzle
like a grainy scene on an old

television, tinny antenna
bent skyward—a steeple,

and I'm standing in the center
of the world, a burning heart,

all around me the smell
of manure I've come to love.

Between Horses

Through still air above the meadow
        stallions plunge into their separate minds

among the white-bearded violets.
        Deep blue marks of sky between horses—

you refuse to wash your hair,
        your feet. The clouds never leave,

are held in constant suspension.
        Nobody calls. No one with power

to adjust the past. It's like the sea,
        how you can only continue,

though creation—hyacinth and earth—
        depends on flesh, on the beginning

of grief. You see your image
        within each horse's frothing mane,

your lawless body a tree.

Sundown, Looking at My Estranged Cousin's
High School Yearbook Picture
and All the Damage Done

No moon tonight but the white bells of a woman's
      eyes squinting tacitly toward a camera, staring out

from the glossy page of a high school yearbook
      on a spring evening that stings like the elegy

of lifting a woman's hair from the shower drain, dredged deep
      in the tiny, aluminum hole you hadn't scrubbed

until now. Now you ask yourself how
      she is here, because you assumed. No moon but stories

of country girls baking strudel in Bad Soden
      in the middle of dawn when everything looks

as if about to catch fire, sky an oblivion appearing
      out of nowhere as they braid dough into

bone-clean rows. What's the point
      of raw ingredients without knowing how to organize

and carry forward? I rinse tomato crust
      from the rims of soup bowls, the metal pot, and imagine,

for the first time, myself in the setting that made me,
      the woman in the picture pressing fingers tightly into mine,

nails almost cutting into joints, leading me through the rubble.

      I keep hearing how caution is a survival skill because no-

                          body knows

what next worse thing is coming. Some nights my neighbor

      texts me, *I love ya*, because I placed her medicine package

outside her apartment door. The day we met there was a power outage

      and I was drunk in the afternoon, brushing my hair.

Former German Broker
Happy as a Farmer Here

Before the farm:
golden, loose-

tongued cows hovering
the feed bunk, grass

green as an apple's
skin. Before

New York
there were carrots

rooted in the ground
in Wiesbaden

flaming and arrogant
as though they could

not be severed.

Regardless, a Bat Mitzvah'd
Woman Cannot Make Minion

FAIR LAWN, NJ

What these girls did I could not: black tights
in June, knowing which spoon for goat's milk,
which for slow-cooked stew, pray from right
to left. Grace: the way they prayed
in long sleeves in sunlight, hair
like wet grass, clean palms warm and pale
as bread. I know now what I meant to ask:
Can I touch your hand, though what I did
was bite. There must be a word for the lack
of words for the things we have felt all
our lives, but couldn't name, a name
for the hymn that moves our blood,
old and dire, like the rain
that once shined each green blade
of that town, not each girl, but the grass
that blooms and blooms and blooms.

It Can't Be Taken

You've spent all day with her
wandering the cornfield, drinking rum
from Coke bottles, trash talking
your fathers—hers
wheelchair bound in Haifa, maybe
peering at the garden, smoking a joint,
bitter, perhaps humming a list in his head
of all the women he's ever slept beside
until morning cracked the old
spell open, yoke cracked onto a spoon.
Your father is on a surgery table up the highway,
anesthetized, the room smelling of oranges
and burning hair, of cutting through bone.
It's beautiful here, she says, as she peels
off her Wrangler jeans and you both
lie down inside a chronic row of corn.
Evening, and you're both so drunk
she pissed herself and the hilarity
of the moment is almost monumental,
though, of course rapture, of course a body
blurting out what's extraneous. She tosses
her pants toward another plot of urine-
colored corn and you are glad
she's beside you, as she's always
been when the whole tapestry
screws itself into the heart's hollering
or its burning.

You remember all the evenings
with her in summer, just like this,
when the shouting flourished
like a box of chives erupting,
you'd walk the mile to meet her
at Dunkin' Donuts—past midnight,
stars hunting you down—
or you'd jump the fence
to the private pool
for a night swim
in the good part of town,
and you love this town
despite what it's come to stand for.

Up the highway, your father is waking
from oblivion, tongue depressor
in his mouth. It is like a new bird waking
from the mouth of her shell.
He can't appreciate it,
but you know there are other contexts
where the big themes pan out.
You've watched her, dead
center of the cornfield,
and it can't be taken,
her body bold
with moonlight, laid bare.

When Will You Learn
There Isn't a Word for Everything?

White fog. Crown of rugged trees. Lilies in the street. Gas stations'
rainbow-oiled cars, people
rushing toward air: thunder-red flames make a lot of beauty
the critical moment
you are meant to answer a call

then pause stupid girl
the broken glass of your brain
next year brother on the bridge nothing
to shake him out of the oldest
dream how we are torn
and whole only in the bird's
head her song in the desert, the payphone
ringing for its life. White fog.

A Blessing, Again or My Grandfather Chooses Against Getting a Pacemaker

The wild leaves have loosened along
the town's avenue where my grandfather
leans, soft-shouldered, against the cracking
brick wall of his sporting goods shop,
sunken eyes squinting in the white orb
of October light, a calloused hand
reaching for something living
outside of the frame. The farm
where his boyhood was buried
is now a blue thread of smoke,
a caged-off landscape of quavering bone.
Autumn will never be infinite, but rather,
an omen—the weight of goldcrests
sucking the legs of pale spiders before
they swallow, breathing in
the stomach muscles, silk glands.
All season he lies to my mother
about his arteries clogging, frail
valves regurgitating. The blood
in his heart is leaking as though
blood is water sliding slowly
down the spine from wet hair
after plunging in a cold and gleaming
stream when he was just a boy.

Elegy for Selma Meerbaum-Eisinger

While you were singing, fall arrived. Yellow leaf
      clipped from your ear. While you were singing,
a forest of beech trees drenched in soldiers, someone
      rearranging the peaches, the deer. Here's
an hour, there's a day. A star
      for your grieving, while you are singing. A rainbow
lives in the throat of the Gods, landlords of Earth, your leaf-eyed
                            season
      cast over a tenantless world—girl at the threshold
catching the light with her hands.

Gustav Barmann, Who Has Put Extensive Alterations on Historic Pine Lane Farm, Contrasts our Freedom with Regimentation in Reich

MIDDLETOWN TIMES HERALD, MIDDLETOWN, NY

DECEMBER 29, 1937

I.

Air shuffles the white flowers of decades ago, a blue wind in the

necks of iron mountains.

You can imagine what the dreams were like: beautiful Eastern

apples—

skin-blushing suns of the apple men, meat animals pedestalled in

the cattle market,

dealers rattling the price. A good business, two brothers shaking

hands in a street

in Wiesbaden, that famous German watering place on the Rhine.

II.

Mountains gauzy with snow, the idea of a spiral staircase to the

                                                other life.

You don't wake. You lie still and listen to your brother's shadow

                                        thistleing the halls,

slim territory of his body timed like a song on a radio.

Tomorrow, the market fruits and bitter rinds of oranges peeled

                                            like confetti.

Mountain with two alphabets and a staircase.

Brother with the dove in his mouth.

III.

The father and mother both studied English
in their own school days:

Milch/milk, *Hertz*/heart—

As it is the way with all of us,
they have forgotten, letters
unfurling into ancient shreds

like their *Stammbaum*, my bloodline.

IV.

The brother is still
in Wiesbaden

but he, too, may not
continue there

indefinitely,
such is the pressure

under which he must
live and work.

V.

Night sky royal as her plumage,
the half-eaten heart of the starling

falls haphazardly from the mountain ash.
A biting stillness enters the daughter and son

like a past. This, the lion's hour—
royal, illiterate bird, the bones frail as ice.

VI.

My sister and I like it here very much,
says the son, his cheeks
rose-colored, soft apples.

Winter's icy wind streams
through the trees' skinned branches.

Perhaps we will forget after a while
those children in our school in Wiesbaden
who used to throw stones at us
because we were Jews.

IV

The Recursive

Last October my father
withered in bed next to the parakeet,
the carpet smothered in bird shit.
On the steps of my favorite cathedral,
I repeated *fuck you*
to an ex who was not there.
Not even the water, churning forever
in the river's holiest mouth,
would envy me. I was hungry
for nothing—the tongue,
thrilled to be cleaved, the sound
of a clock becoming his name.

Reading *Odi et Amo* After Going to the Bronx Zoo

Nearly an architecture with all its verbs in place, two arks
       touching lightly above the water, nearly dark
as you reach for the window, flowers out of focus
       in the waves. There were years you couldn't speak,
your pigeon-toed tongue. A strong wind. Behind you
       the past grows louder, nearly the elephants fleeing,
nearly lions. Tomorrow
       you will take a walk. Tomorrow you will mail a letter.
There is a dream emerging from the river, the animals
       rushing toward their names.

I've Been Living for a Long Time
on the Bottom of Rivers

They kill the sitting red fox
       at the shooting range it is nothing—
a red plastic sticker though still

       when I position my rifle
I puke all over my purple
       child's-coat red earmuffs

the sound

       something buried something
learning to hear underwater
       the sound is teeth shaking

collar bone bruising in the night
       I memorize the spot like a headache
that night I'm still a girl

       barefoot on grass the neighbors waving
a cane in my father's face *Kikes* they yell
       the night shrieks frozen

he runs hungrily to offer his coat.

Your Heart Flies into My Head

I was born in a month I couldn't touch
      the pretty roofs brown leaves icing houses

I sat my teenage years in the bathroom sink
      cracked egg on my face toothpaste smudged

my knees the mirror got me sick
      a town is its own mirror

pretty oak maple sycamore
      drug store pork store video store

that insane house beneath the pathetic clouds
      October your heart flies into my head.

Infinity Room

Sometimes the galaxy I drew while sitting
on the purple carpet of my mother's girlhood
room lacked planets, though it was possessed
by silver ocean, a few red fish. Sometimes
it was a field, simple, with a wooden bench,
where a girl sucks rosewater from a fissure
in the frame. After my grandmother's death,
it took one week to gut the house. On the third night,
horses freaked in their limitations. I opened
a wooden chest of old Polaroids. By the seventh,
I had no idea what I was doing in Brooklyn—
land of Great Aunt Girdy's beach.
It doesn't matter if the story
happened this way, only that it's what's left
and goes on. In the new architecture,
I draw myself standing in my Grandmother's
attic folding my mother's old dresses inside
a life-sized Ziploc bag. Like a good daughter
I toss the boxes of broken plates
into the town dump. Evening sun
glistens like cantaloupe. I travel
room to room pillaging the drawers
for Polaroids to cram in my purse.
I never see the faces on them again.
Walking Brighton Beach boardwalk:
wooden plank, bicycle wheel, wind grappling
a pink umbrella. Polaroids ringing the axis
of my purse like a family of planets.

Great Aunt Girdy, blue two-piece,
wading the surf. Somehow, American.
Did she appear tall among the massive
body of ocean. Did my family ever
speak to one another. Did she
look attractive or Jewish.

Ungenesis

I was young, a myth, chewing
the apple. I slept in a hemisphere
of coats pushing out of the flames.
Every city burns, I know,
though I'm not a mystic.
There are so many ways to be
betrayed by a country—
my ancestors—goat bones,
stars in the butcher's thumb.
They live in the milky river
that surges through the mountain
burdened with our names.

Kabbalah for Last November

This is the afternoon the women dance on the grassy hill, unclothed
        and untethered as the wolves of Belarus, before the word

for water appears like a seed of the aftermath, before the lesson
        of numbers darkens. One woman stretches her shining torso

into the weather, extends the reach of her palm,
        safe for a second from the dead

of winter revealing its prophecy in the almond tree. Another
        falls backward into matte-blue sky.

You can't see her face, can't distinguish
        pain from healing. You have dragged your chair up here

to learn desire in the movement of muscles bulbous beneath skin,
        each woman her own unholy architecture, hair blooming

wild behind her. You have always been the woman in the flooding
        room, refusing to move out of the way.

Neo-Romanticism

I am no longer the same now
walking the beach in early morning
just after the dredgers have gone.
Sand smooth as though something
holy has vanished. Last night a couple
fell asleep in a pink motel
with split ends and forgetting skins.
All my life I have wanted to
be immense, thoroughly a self.
I have wished to ask for nothing
or at the very least that when I pray
the store-bought streamers
of language would be rid of men.
Of course, it is logical to look toward
a body at this hour. I am
looking for God. It's not romantic.
I can't rescind your name.

Animal Dressed in the Skin of Your Silence

I am permitted to know only the garden,
        the pond, a mesh of fish silvering downstream.

Fingers pressed in mud, in this world I imagine
        my dead cousins dancing in a landscape

of lavas and basalts, glowing stone
        from the world's heart. I stare into

the sixteen petals of the Daphne.
        In this world, I bathe only

in a porcelain tub, the pipes
        clogged with wet earth, water filtered

from a landscape of furious heat.
        I imagine I can imagine cousins.

        The water rises. The steam rises.

Will I ever stop being angry
        for never hearing my family's language?

In every city,
        every spit-shined field,

I hear the violet, ancient noise
        of my family's silence. The silence

shimmers. It is forged the way Earth's magma
        is made into glimmering rock.

This rock will furnish
        the future's room.

Giving the Names of Things Their Solitude

I don't remember when I began hearing
a tune in the rain and architecture
but nights are so tranquil now
like floating in seawater, the teal broth
making room for me, a minor planet.
I float through my weeks listening
to birds lifting from the sable lottery
of city trash bags, glad to be far away
from your voice, undisturbed by speech.
I have always cared too much for the idea
that two animals who have minds,
an aptitude for thought, are meant
to understand and take care of each other.
Even in failure it's something I demanded—
a virtuoso demanding eloquence
from a smashed flute. Through the twilight
spring's pink blossoms give
themselves away. I'm not sorry if we never
speak again—the exaggerated squirrels,
their kissing bones, and tearing through soil
the raw sounds of the new world.

NOTES

The title "A Blessing" is indebted to James Wright and the line "(opened / or closed)" in this poem is borrowed from Sharon Olds.

The italicized lines in the poem "Grandfather Reading Celan in Middletown, NY" are translations of Paul Celan by Pierre Joris from *Breathturn into Timestead*.

The line "the soft hurricanes of running feet" and phrase "woolly-leafed" in "Ocean Liner to the United States, 1935" are from Pablo Neruda's *The Heights of Macchu Picchu*, translated by Tomás Q. Morín.

The sequence "Gustav Barmann, Who Has Put Extensive Alterations on Historic Pine Lane Farm, Contrasts our Freedom with Regimentation in Reich" also carries inspiration from Pablo Neruda and borrows language from a newspaper article about my family's immigration story published in the *Middletown Times Herald* in 1937. "Former German Broker Happy as a Farmer Here" also borrows language from this newspaper article.

The title "Sundown, Looking at My Estranged Cousin's High School Yearbook Picture and All the Damage Done," is inspired by Ada Limón. This poem also draws inspiration from Lucie Brock-Broido.

Selma Meerbaum-Eisinger was a Jewish poet and younger cousin of Paul Celan. Both were born in Cernăuți, Romania (now Czernowitz), and wrote in German. She died of typhus in the Nazi SS labor camp Michailowka in Ukraine in 1942. She was eighteen years old.

The poems "I've Been Living for a Long Time on the Bottom of Rivers" and "Your Heart Flies into My Head" are inspired by Sarah Kirsch.

"Animal Dressed in the Skin of Your Silence" is inspired by Paul Celan.

ACKNOWLEDGMENTS

Thank you to the editors of the following publications who have published poems from this collection, sometimes in different forms:

Action/Spectacle, *The Abandoned Playground*, *Bennington Review*, *The Common*, *Epiphany Literary Magazine*, *Four Way Review*, *Kenyon Review*, *Los Angeles Review of Books Quarterly (LARB)*, *Narrative Magazine*, *North American Review, Poetry Northwest*, *Salmagundi*, *Smartish Pace*, *Through Lines Magazine*, and *Tupelo Quarterly*.

Thank you to Martha Rhodes, Ryan Murphy, Hannah Matheson, Jonathan Blunk, and the entire brilliant team at Four Way Books for your belief, support, insight, and ingenuity.

Thank you to Johnny Steers for being who you are. Thank you to Ariel Francisco Henriquez Cos (mostly here; always there), Marci Calabretta Cancio-Bello, Michelle Delaney, Devin Gael Kelly, and Binnie Kirshenbaum.

This book is for my mother, Barbara Cecille Barmann Hoffman, and my late grandfather, Kurt Barmann, whom I speak to here through the stories handed down.

PUBLICATION OF THIS BOOK WAS MADE POSSIBLE
BY GRANTS AND DONATIONS. WE ARE ALSO GRATEFUL
TO THOSE INDIVIDUALS WHO PARTICIPATED IN
OUR 2022 BUILD A BOOK PROGRAM. THEY ARE:

Anonymous (12), Robert Abrams, Michael Ansara, Kathy
Aponick, Jean Ball, Sally Ball, Clayre Benzadón, Adrian
Blevins, Laurel Blossom, adam bohannon, Betsy Bonner,
Patricia Bottomley, Lee Briccetti, Joel Brouwer, Susan
Buttenwieser, Anthony Cappo, Paul and Brandy Carlson,
Mark Conway, Elinor Cramer, Dan and Karen Clarke, Kwame
Dawes, Michael Anna de Armas, John Del Peschio, Brian
Komei Dempster, Rosalynde Vas Dias, Patrick Donnelly, Lynn
Emanuel, Blas Falconer, Jennifer Franklin, John Gallaher,
Reginald Gibbons, Rebecca Kaiser Gibson, Dorothy Tapper
Goldman, Julia Guez, Naomi Guttman and Jonathan Mead,
Forrest Hamer, Luke Hankins, Yona Harvey, KT Herr, Karen
Hildebrand, Carlie Hoffman, Glenna Horton, Thomas and
Autumn Howard, Catherine Hoyser, Elizabeth Jackson, Linda
Susan Jackson, Jessica Jacobs and Nickole Brown, Lee Jenkins,
Elizabeth Kanell, Nancy Kassell, Maeve Kinkead, Victoria
Korth, Brett Lauer and Gretchen Scott, Howard Levy, Owen
Lewis and Susan Ennis, Margaree Little, Sara London and
Dean Albarelli, Tariq Luthun, Myra Malkin, Louise Mathias,
Victoria McCoy, Lupe Mendez, Michael and Nancy Murphy,
Kimberly Nunes, Susan Okie and Walter Weiss, Cathy
McArthur Palermo, Veronica Patterson, Jill Pearlman, Marcia
and Chris Pelletiere, Sam Perkins, Susan Peters and Morgan
Driscoll, Maya Pindyck, Megan Pinto, Kevin Prufer, Martha
Rhodes, Paula Rhodes, Louise Riemer, Peter and Jill Schireson,
Rob Schlegel, Yoana Setzer, Soraya Shalforoosh, Mary Slechta,

Diane Souvaine, Barbara Spark, Catherine Stearns, Jacob
Strautmann, Yerra Sugarman, Arthur Sze and Carol Moldaw,
Marjorie and Lew Tesser, Dorothy Thomas, Rushi Vyas, Martha
Webster and Robert Fuentes, Rachel Weintraub and Allston
James, Jane and Jonathan Wells, Abigail Wender, D. Wolff, and
Monica Youn.